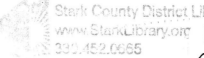

INSIDE MARTIAL ARTS

MIXED
MARTIAL ARTS

by Annabelle Tometich

Content Consultant:
Nick "The Goat" Thompson
Minnesota Martial Arts Academy

SportsZone
An Imprint of Abdo Publishing | www.abdopublishing.com

www.abdopublishing.com

Published by Abdo Publishing, a division of ABDO, PO Box 398166, Minneapolis, Minnesota 55439. Copyright © 2015 by Abdo Consulting Group, Inc. International copyrights reserved in all countries. No part of this book may be reproduced in any form without written permission from the publisher. SportsZone™ is a trademark and logo of Abdo Publishing.

Printed in the United States of America, North Mankato, Minnesota
102014
012015

Cover Photo: David Becker/AP Images
Interior Photos: David Becker/AP Images, 1, 40; Jeff Chiu/AP Images, 4–5, 7, 12–13, 26, 29 (top), 30–31, 32; The Canadian Press, Jonathan Hayward/AP Images, 8; imago sportfotodienst/Newscom, 10; Darryl Dennis/Icon SMI/Newscom, 14, 16, 20–21, 22; Rogan Thomson/ActionPlus/Newscom, 19; Eric Jamison/AP Images, 24, 38–39, 43; Matt Strasen/AP Images, 27; Isaac Brekken/AP Images, 28 (top), 29 (bottom); Gregory Payan/AP Images, 28 (bottom), 36; Uwe Anspach/picture-alliance/dpa/AP Images, 34; Tim Larsen/AP Images, 35; Jae C. Hong/AP Images, 44

Editor: Thomas K. Adamson
Series Designer: Becky Daum

Library of Congress Control Number: 2014944201

Cataloging-in-Publication Data
Tometich, Annabelle.
 Mixed martial arts / Annabelle Tometich.
   p. cm. – (Inside martial arts)
ISBN 978-1-62403-605-7 (lib. bdg.)
Includes bibliographical references and index.
1. Mixed martial arts–Juvenile literature.   I. Title.
796.8–dc23   2014944201

TABLE OF CONTENTS

MMA

CHAPTER 1

EPIC BATTLE

Dan Henderson and Mauricio Rua could barely stand. They had fought for five rounds in a mixed martial arts (MMA) match. They were exhausted. Henderson had broken his thumb. Rua had suffered a possible skull fracture. The fighters had exchanged punches and kicks. They had wrestled each other to the mat. They had smashed each other into the cage surrounding the ring.

Dan Henderson, *top*, fights Mauricio Rua in a UFC 139 bout.

Henderson and Rua were competing in the Ultimate Fighting Championship (UFC). The event was UFC 139. It took place on November 19, 2011, in San Jose, California. Both fighters had won MMA championships. Both had defeated strong opponents to get to this championship match. On this day, they were evenly matched.

Rua landed the first strike to start the match. It was a low kick. Henderson answered with hard punches to Rua's head. Throughout the match, the fighters hit with their elbows. They grappled on the mat.

Every time one fighter seemed in control, the other came back. By the end, Rua and Henderson were bleeding. Their faces were swollen. They were so tired they could barely hold their arms up.

The judges named Henderson the winner. He won by one point. He called it one of the toughest fights of his life. It is considered one of the greatest MMA fights of all time.

Dan Henderson, *left*, and Mauricio Rua, *right*,
were exhausted from the long, bloody fight.

MMA combines moves from all of the combat and martial arts sports. MMA fighters use the kicks of karate. They use throws and chokes like judo fighters. They punch and hit like boxers. They grapple like wrestlers.

MMA fighters have to learn techniques from many different fighting styles. They have to be strong and tough. They cannot be afraid of getting hit.

Different forms of MMA have been around for centuries. In 648 BC, the ancient Greeks wrote about *pankration*. Pankration meant "all powers." It combined the skills of boxing and wrestling. Pankration matches were brutal. The fighters could do almost anything to their opponents.

Fighters often battled to the death. Those who won were treated like heroes. Artists carved their images into stone.

MMA fighters use kicks in addition to punches, throws, and chokes.

Dioxippus was a legendary pankration fighter. He trained the Greek and Roman armies in combat. Some believe these armies spread pankration throughout Europe and into China. Pankration could be the basis for Asia's martial arts.

In the late 1800s, submission wrestling became popular in the United States. Submission wrestlers used holds and joint locks. These moves created pain. The pain eventually made opponents quit. In 1914, legendary submission wrestler Ad Santel went to Japan. He defeated two of the best judo fighters in the world. His moves fascinated the Japanese.

Japanese fighters with backgrounds in judo, sumo, karate, and kickboxing learned to wrestle. Eventually, the styles combined. They started fighting using a mix of martial arts.

In 1914, famous judo teacher Mitsuyo Maeda traveled to Brazil. He went to spread the sport of judo. Maeda met Gastao Gracie. Maeda offered to teach Gracie's sons, Carlos

Competitions called pankration are similar to MMA.

and Helio, judo and jujutsu. They proved to be excellent students, especially Helio.

Helio was smaller. He held opponents with his legs. He waited for them to make mistakes. Helio also developed new techniques. He taught them to his students. This was the start of Brazilian jiujitsu.

Helio fought champions in boxing, wrestling, and karate. He also taught the Gracie form of jiujitsu to his seven sons. They then spread it around the world, including the United States.

In 1993, Helio's son Rorion and his brothers held a tournament. They wanted to find the best martial art. They brought together fighters of all types. There were sumo wrestlers, boxers, kickboxers, and karate champions. The matches were held in a caged ring. They called it the Ultimate Fighting Championship.

The UFC is the largest MMA promotion company in the world. It has spread MMA to more than 150 countries. It has given this ancient sport a new and modern life.

THE GRACIE CHALLENGE

Helio Gracie wanted to prove that his form of jiujitsu was the best. He invited fighters in all martial arts to fight him. His invitation became known as the Gracie Challenge. Helio's sons kept the Challenge alive. His son Rorion offered $100,000 to any fighter who could beat him. Fighters from all over the world accepted his Gracie Challenge. It made the Gracie brothers famous worldwide.

CHAPTER 2
TECHNIQUES AND MOVES

MMA has always been a tough sport. The first UFC matches were especially brutal. In UFC 1, fighters broke fingers. They knocked out teeth. They suffered concussions. Early UFC fights led to a set of rules for the sport.

Famed jiujitsu fighter Royce Gracie won the first UFC in 1993. He was the brother of the event's organizer, Rorion

MMA is a tough sport. Fighters have to be ready to take punches.

Royce Gracie, *left*, pictured here during a fight in 2007, was
the champion of the first Ultimate Fighting Championship.

Gracie, and a grandson of Helio Gracie. Royce wore a martial

arts uniform, called a *gi*, in his fights. In one fight, Royce

used his gi to choke Ken Shamrock and make him submit.

Shamrock was one of the most feared fighters of the time.

The audience thought Royce's win was staged. They thought his opponents were not good enough. They thought referees stopped the action too soon. In response, Royce and Rorion set up another UFC competition.

The Gracies wanted to make this UFC memorable. They wanted to get rid of referees. They were going to leave the fighters alone in the ring. They said matches would end by knockout, submission, or death.

This idea was a little too extreme. Some people wanted the fights stopped. So the Gracies hired a referee named "Big John" McCarthy. Big John trained police officers in combat. He had been to crime scenes. He knew jiujitsu. He did not mind blood. Big John's job was to watch over the fighters. He would make sure they fought fair. But he was not allowed to stop matches even if a fighter was getting badly beaten. Big John did not like this rule.

In a bout at UFC 2, Patrick Smith pinned fighter Scott Morris to the mat. Smith unleashed elbows and punches to

Morris's head. Morris was barely conscious. He was in no shape to continue fighting. He was so out of it that he could not even tap out, or submit, on his own.

Big John was not allowed to stop the match. He looked on helplessly as Morris took hit after hit. Smith finally realized how badly he had hurt Morris. Smith stopped the fight himself. Morris stumbled out of the ring. He never fought in another UFC match.

Big John told Rorion he would never again be a UFC referee. He said he did not want to watch someone get killed. Rorion agreed. He gave Big John the power to stop fights. But only if a fighter was in serious danger.

MMA has come a long way since UFC 1 and 2. Fighters must now follow a set of rules for fighting. They are known as the Unified Rules of Mixed Martial Arts. These rules are used in most MMA fights. The rules allow for 10 weight

Big John McCarthy insisted on having the power to stop fights if a fighter was in serious danger.

classes. Weight classes range from flyweight (116 to 125 pounds) to heavyweight (206 to 265 pounds).

Unlike when Royce Gracie fought, MMA fighters cannot wear gis. Male fighters cannot wear shirts of any kind. Shoes are also not allowed.

The Unified Rules allow grappling, submission holds, kicking, and striking. The rules ban unfair moves that may seriously injure a fighter. Head butting, eye gouging, biting, spitting, and clawing are not allowed. Strikes to the groin, spine, back of the head, and throat are also illegal. Fighters may not kick, knee, or stomp on an opponent who is on the ground.

The Unified Rules set standards for MMA rings and cages. MMA rings are similar to boxing rings. They have ropes, poles, and padded floors. MMA fights usually occur in cages, though. MMA cages must be circular or have at least six sides. UFC cages are always octagons. They are usually

The cage for UFC fights is an octagon.

enclosed by a chain-link fence. Cages are between 20 feet

(6 m) and 32 feet (9.8 m) wide.

The ring's size gives fighters enough room to make their

moves. The cage keeps fighters from escaping. The cage

forces action. Audiences love action.

MMA is not as brutal and bloody as it was in 1993.

But it remains a sport that requires incredible toughness,

strength, and determination.

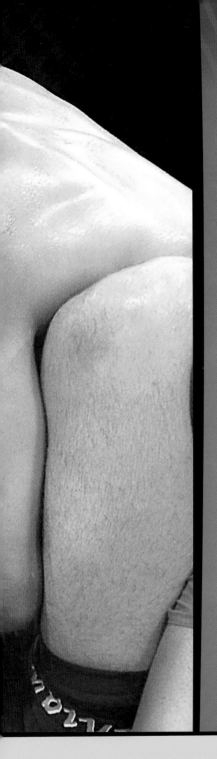

CHAPTER 3
TRAINING

UFC 1 and 2 proved that grappling skills are key to MMA success. Royce Gracie won both events by wrestling his opponents to the mat. He then wrapped their limbs in painful holds. His opponents were not tired. But he forced them to tap out.

Boxers and karate fighters do not train to fight from their backs. They always stand up during their matches and avoid falling down. This gave Royce

MMA fighters have to be able to fight while lying on the mat.

Phillip Brown has Nick Quintong in a choke hold.

a major advantage. He could fight on the ground like a

wrestler. He could throw punches like a boxer.

Royce showed the world a new type of fighting. His form

of MMA required a variety of skills. To take Royce down,

fighters would have to train as he did. They would have to master many different martial arts.

MMA fighters devote much of their practice to ground work. They learn to grapple. They learn how to perform holds. These techniques force opponents to tap out. They can end a match quickly. The three main holds are chokes, arm locks, and leg locks.

In a choke, a fighter applies pressure to the opponent's neck. Chokes restrict blood flow to the brain. This will cause the opponent to pass out. Most fighters tap out before passing out.

With locks, a fighter wraps up an opponent's arm or leg. The fighter then bends or twists the joints. From there, the fighter applies incredible pressure to the elbows, knees, wrists, ankles, or feet. The pressure makes it feel like the joint is going to break. This intense pain causes opponents to tap out.

Dustin Poirier makes Max Holloway tap out with an arm lock.

Fighters train to defend against holds. They learn to not leave themselves vulnerable. When fighters cannot apply holds, they resort to strikes. Strikes include punches and kicks. Fighters can also use their knees, elbows, and forearms for strikes. Strikes weaken opponents. Blows to the head make it hard for an opponent to see and think. A well-placed strike can knock out an opponent and end the fight quickly. But a fighter defending against a strike may become the victim of a hold.

MMA fighters must learn to throw strikes from all angles. They learn to hit and kick while standing. They learn to strike while on their backs and off balance. They also learn to strike while on top of an opponent.

Many of the great MMA fighters got started in wrestling. Wrestling teaches a fighter to control his or her opponent's body. It is a crucial skill in MMA. UFC Hall

THE TWISTER

The "twister" is one of the most painful MMA locks. It has only been used once in a UFC competition. In 2011, Chan Sung Jung made Leonard Garcia submit with a twister. Jung hooked one of Garcia's legs. He then grabbed Garcia's head. Jung twisted Garcia's leg and body one way. He cranked his head the other way. The move put huge pressure on Garcia's spine. Garcia tapped out with just one second left in the match.

of Fame fighter Dan Severn won his first match without throwing a single punch. Royce Gracie threw very few strikes in his UFC career.

MMA fighters try to get on top of an opponent and then rain down punches.

Jessica Andrade lands a punch against Raquel Pennington.

An MMA fighter must be well-rounded to win. MMA cannot be learned through studying alone. A great fighter must have skills and toughness. Gracie believed toughness was taught in the ring.

MMA MOVES

Punches

MMA fighters throw punches like boxers do.

Leg Lock

A leg lock can make an opponent tap out from the pain of the twisted joint.

Choke

A choke hold puts pressure on the opponent's neck, forcing a tap out. Both locks and chokes are taken from jiujitsu.

Kicks

A well-placed kick is another weapon fighters use. Kicking moves come from the combat sport Muay Thai.

CHAPTER 4
ADVANCED MMA

MMA fighters must have tough bodies and tough minds. Former UFC champion Rich Franklin once said that training is 90 percent physical. But fighting is 90 percent mental.

MMA fighters cannot be afraid of getting hit. They cannot be afraid of being thrown to the ground. The best MMA fighters are always looking

Josh Thomson throws Bobby Green to the mat.

Anderson Silva kicks Chael Sonnen during their 2010 match.

for opportunities. They try to get back up after being knocked down.

In August 2010, Anderson Silva faced Chael Sonnen. Sonnen dominated four of the five rounds. He struck Silva 278 times. Silva had just 54 strikes. Silva looked hopeless.

In the fifth and final round, Sonnen rained punches down on Silva. Silva let him gain confidence. Just when

Sonnen seemed the clear winner, Silva struck. He grabbed Sonnen's wrist. He shot his legs around Sonnen's neck. He caught Sonnen's left arm against his leg. He pulled the arm backward. He forced Sonnen to tap out. There were less than two minutes left in the fight.

The win confirmed Silva to be one of the greatest MMA fighters of all time. It proved a fight is not over until the very end.

Silva was born in Brazil. He trains five and a half hours a day leading up to fights. He spars. He does cardio exercises. He builds strength. Silva trains in boxing and jiujitsu. He trains in tae kwon do and Muay Thai, a martial art similar to kickboxing. He also trains in capoeira. Capoeira is a Brazilian martial art. It combines dance, acrobatics, and music. Dancing may sound like an odd way to train. But capoeira requires rhythm and strength. It teaches fighters to be agile. It also teaches flexibility.

Silva credits this diverse training for his success in MMA. Through 2013, Silva had the most knockdowns in UFC history. He had the most consecutive wins too, with 17. He defended his middleweight championship 10 times.

However, in December 2013 Silva broke his leg during a UFC fight. MMA fighters must deal with serious injuries. Broken bones and concussions are common dangers.

Because injuries happen often in MMA, the UFC works hard to protect the health of its fighters. A fighter who

Fighters train with striking pads.

MMA fighters take multiple blows to the head during every fight.

suffers a concussion, even a minor one, is suspended for

three months by the UFC. The fighter cannot train in combat

drills for at least 60 days. Concussions occur when the brain

bounces around inside the skull. This usually happens after

a big hit or strike. Concussions sometimes mean a fighter

is knocked out. But a fighter may appear OK despite having

a concussion. Concussions affect the way fighters think

and act. The fighters do not even realize how much danger

Doctors are nearby at every fight to tend to injuries after the fight is over.

they are in. Concussions make it hard for fighters to defend themselves smartly.

Even small blows to the head may impact a fighter's health. Repeated head injuries can lead to brain damage and memory loss. They have also been linked to depression. Fighters must be careful to protect themselves.

Suspensions are not only for concussions. UFC organizers impose strict suspensions for broken bones and other serious injuries. Doctors stand ringside for all UFC fights. They look for injuries. They can force an injured fighter to leave a bout. Since UFC started in 1993, through 2014, there has never been a death or paralyzing injury.

MMA fighters must learn to absorb kicks and punches. MMA coaches often punch their fighters. They punch them over and over again. They teach them not to be afraid of hits. Fighters are taught to see the punches coming. They put their chins down. They absorb punches with their foreheads. The bone in the forehead is harder than others around the face.

Great MMA fighters know how to create pain. They also know how to take it. When fighters can do both, they are ready for competition.

EQUIPMENT

All MMA fighters need the right equipment to compete. They use a mouthpiece, lightweight gloves, approved shorts, and hand wraps. Men must wear groin protectors. They cannot wear shirts. Women must wear approved chest coverings.

CHAPTER 5
COMPETITIONS

MMA fighters train hard. It can be years before they are ready for competition.

Non-championship MMA fights last three rounds. Championship fights go five rounds. Rounds last no more than five minutes. There is a one-minute rest between rounds. Fights are started and stopped by referees.

The referee pushes Lyoto Machida away after Machida knocked out Thiago Silva.

Demian Maia celebrates after knocking down Dong Hyun Kim.

In MMA fights, winners are determined by submission, knockout, or judges' decision.

In a submission, the opponent taps out. He or she can tap out verbally. They can also tap out by physically tapping the fighter or the mat.

A true knockout is known as a KO. A KO happens when an opponent is rendered unconscious due to strikes or kicks. If a referee stops the match, then that is a technical knockout (TKO). A fighter can also win by TKO if their opponent breaks the rules.

Three judges watch each MMA bout. The judges score each round. Scores are based on how well each opponent fights. The judges watch from different locations. They are looking for good striking and grappling. They are also looking for fighters with control. They look for aggression. The judges are looking for good defense too. If there is no knockout or submission, then these scores are totaled to determine the winner.

Judges use a 10-point system. The winner of a round earns 10 points. The loser earns nine points or fewer. The loser's score depends on their performance.

Judges can reach three types of decisions. A unanimous decision is when all three judges pick the same winner.

A split decision is when two judges pick one fighter, and one judge picks the other. There can also be a majority decision. That's when two judges pick one fighter and one judge scores the bout as a draw.

Fighters who break the rules commit fouls. A fighter can be disqualified for too many fouls or one serious foul. Fighters can also lose points for fouls.

Fighters start in amateur matches. They then apply for professional fights. Promoters pick fighters for pro bouts based on their records. They look for fighters with experience. Pro fighters compete for money. Once a fighter turns pro, he or she can no longer compete against amateurs.

Fighters can apply to be in the UFC once they get some pro wins. Fighters send in videos of their bouts. UFC officials watch the videos. If they think the fighter's skills are good enough for the UFC, they will pick the fighter to be in an event.

Quinton Jackson, *right*, lands a knockout
punch against Wanderlei Silva.

In 2013, the UFC had 475 fighters, including 29 female
fighters. The UFC hosted 33 fighting events that year. In
2014, the UFC hosted more than 40 fighting events. UFC
fighters can fight twice a year to five times a year or more.
That number depends on injuries and other factors.

Ronda Rousey gets ready for an MMA fight.

UFC is the largest and most popular MMA promotion company in the world. But it is not the only one. The World Series of Fighting (WSOF) started in 2012. Its fights take place in a 10-sided ring, or decagon. The WSOF follows the same rules as the UFC.

MMA companies like One Fighting Championship are popular in Asia. Bellator MMA started in the US in 2008.

Several of its fighters have gone on to the UFC. Invicta Fighting Championships promotes women's MMA fights.

The best MMA fighters can win millions of dollars. They become superstars. In 2013, UFC president Dana White said the company had paid as much as $5 million to a single fighter. That was for just one bout. MMA champions have starred in Hollywood movies. They have thousands of fans.

It takes brute strength and toughness to be an MMA fighter. Sometimes it pays to be tough.

THE ULTIMATE FIGHTER

A reality TV show might have saved the UFC. UFC president Dana White helped develop *The Ultimate Fighter*. This show began in 2004. It showed how fighters train and live. Viewers got to see the extremely hard work that goes into MMA fighting. *The Ultimate Fighter* brought MMA to millions of people and made it a valuable business. In 2001, White and his business partners bought the UFC for $2 million. In 2014, White estimated the UFC was worth $3.5 billion.

GLOSSARY

amateur
An athlete who has never competed for payment.

cardio
Exercises such as running and swimming that cause the heart to beat faster.

concussion
Injury to the brain or spinal cord due to a blow or fall.

conscious
Awake with full mental awareness.

grapple
To seize another in a firm grip.

knockdown
To bring a fighter to the mat with a blow.

lock
Grasping and isolating an opponent's limb for submission.

promoter
A person who organizes a sporting event.

referee
A judge who enforces the rules of a sport.

FOR MORE INFORMATION

Further Readings

Gentry, Clyde. *No Holds Barred: The Complete History of Mixed Martial Arts in America*. Chicago, IL: Triumph, 2011.

Kraus, Erich, and Bret Aita. *Brawl: A Behind-the-Scenes Look at Mixed Martial Arts Competition*. Toronto, Canada: ECW, 2002.

Sheridan, Sam. *The Fighter's Mind: Inside the Mental Game*. New York: Atlantic Monthly, 2010.

Snowden, Jonathan. *Total MMA: Inside Ultimate Fighting*. Toronto, Canada: ECW, 2008.

Snowden, Jonathan, and Kendall Shields. *The MMA Encyclopedia*. Toronto, Canada: ECW, 2010.

Websites

To learn more about Inside Martial Arts, visit **booklinks.abdopublishing.com**. These links are routinely monitored and updated to provide the most current information available.

INDEX

ABOUT THE AUTHOR

Annabelle Tometich is an award-winning writer and reporter. She has written several children's books on topics ranging from lacrosse and gymnastics to nutrition and popular culture. Annabelle lives in Fort Myers, Florida, with her husband and their two really cute kids.